Philippians-

The Path of Life
New Testament

JOHN E. NEYMAN, JR., MA., Th.D.

Philippians—The Path to Joy!

The JEN translation is the authors own translation.

Copyright© 2019 by John Neyman and NeymanLLC

All rights reserved. No part of this publication may be reproduced, distributed, or transmitted in any form or by any means, including photocopying, recording, or other electronic or mechanical methods, without the prior written permission of the publisher, except in the case of brief quotations embodied in critical reviews and certain other noncommercial uses permitted by copyright law. For permission requests, write to the publisher, addressed "Attention: Permissions Coordinator," at the address below.

Philippians—The Path to Joy!

Thy word is a lamp unto my feet, and a light unto my path. (Psalm 119:105 KJV)

John Neyman
PO BOX 34 Sarver
PA 16055
www.renewedlifecenter.com

The materials contained in this book are for general information purposes only and do not constitute legal or professional advice on any subject. John E. Neyman or NeymanLLC does not accept any responsibility for any loss or harm which may arise from reliance on information contained in this book.

Philippians—The Path to Joy!

First Print July 10, 2019
RENEWED LIFE COUNSELING CENTER
NEYMAN LLC
PO BOX 34 Sarver, PA 16055 Phone: 724-712-9449 FAX: 724-352-168

This book series is dedicated to Jesus Christ who paid the ultimate sacrifice for His people.

May all of the glory go to Him.

This book—Philippians—The Path to Joy is dedicated to my three children who are a joy to my heart!

Philip
Laura
Matthew

If I could do life over again with them, I would!!

Philippians—The Path to Joy!

Dedication

I would like to thank the Lord Jesus Christ for saving me and calling me into the ministry. He has been extremely faithful to me, which has certainly been unmerited. He has helped me through the most difficult of situations in my life. It is because of Him and the Holy Spirit that I have been able to maintain on the path of Joy! May all of the glory go to Him.

I am thankful for my wife Debbie who loves the Word of God. She promised to take care of me in so many ways and she has truly been faithful to her word.

I am thankful for my three children, Philip, Laura, and Matthew who have maintained loved for me through the thick and thin of life. Parenting does not come with a manual, but God was gracious to help us.

I am thankful for my four stepchildren, Jason, Melissa, Joey, and Jeff. Thank you for accepting me as your stepdad.

There have been so many people in my past who have loved me, taught me, and put up with me. You know who you are. I just want to say thank you so much for all that you have done for me. It has not gone unnoticed. I know that the Lord, Himself, has been keeping good records in order to reward you.

I am also thankful for the challenges that I have had to face in my life through people and circumstances.

All of those challenges have driven me to Christ to find strength, comfort, peace, and renewal. I would never have known what I share in this series without them.

Thank you to everyone for all that you have done for me throughout my life. May God richly bless you all—In Jesus name Amen!

Philippians—The Path to Joy!

The JEN Translation

The JEN translation provides an interpretive meaning of the text. There are various types of translations on the market to help the Body of Christ to understand the Word of God. There are literal translations, translations that provide the ideas of the Greek and Hebrew text, and paraphrases of the text. The JEN text is a translation that conveys interpretive meaning of the text so that there is clarification. The JEN translation will enable you to understand God's Word and the meaning of the text. The author has attempted to italicize all words that have been added to make sense of the text.

The JEN translation is experiencing the power of God with fresh insight and understanding. The footnotes are informative, therapeutic, and instructive. They will encourage you to put the Biblical text into practice. In order to walk in wisdom, you must understand the text, know what it means, and apply the text. The footnotes are both technical and practical that the author hopes you will be able to experience the power of Scripture in your life.

And now bow your head as I bless you with this blessing: ***"May you always walk on the path of Life in His presence, under His authority, and for His glory."***

Philippians—The Path to Joy!

Introduction to Philippians

AUTHOR: Paul

DATE OF WRITING: AD 62

Paul was writing from jail in Rome.

FOUNDING OF THE CHURCH IN PHILIPPI

Paul visited Philippi on his second missionary journey. On that visit, he led to Christ Lydia and her family, the Philippian jailer and his family, and the demon possessed girl (Acts 16:14-34).

The city of Philippi was a Roman colony. It modeled Rome. It was strategically located on an important trade route between Europe and Asia. The city was named after Philip of Macedon, the father of Alexander the Great.

OCCASION

There were several reasons Paul wrote this letter:

- Philippians was thanking the church for gifts they sent.
- There was conflict between two women. He mentioned them by name in 4:1-2.
- There was possible false teaching moving into the church.
- Paul wanted to encourage the church to be joyful.

CHARACTERISTICS

Philippians—The Path to Joy!

The Philippian church was the first church established in Europe. The book of Philippians is characteristically Gentile. Women occupied a prominent place in the church. A woman was the first convert in Europe (Lydia). Paul's first meeting was attended by women (Acts 16:12-15). Two women were prominent in the church (Philippians 4:2).

The church at Philippi was one of the most generous in financial support (4:10-16). Paul presented them as a model of giving (2 Co. 8:1-5). The theme is joy. Joy is used in one form or another seventeen times. Philippians centers upon Christ. In 104 verses, there are fifty-one references to the Lord Jesus by name. There is a lot of personal information about Paul in the epistle. ***Philippians certainly provides us with the Path to Joy!***

KEY VERSE

But even more so, I count all of these things to be a loss because of the superiority of the knowledge of Christ Jesus My Lord. Because of Him, I have disregarded everything, and I count all of my good works as worthless so that I could have Christ…..

Philippians—The Path to Joy!

CHAPTER 1

Introduction

1. From Paul the Apostle and Timothy free slaves of the Lord Jesus Christ. To the Church at Philippi. To all of the church members, the saints in Jesus Christ and to all of the overseers[1]: *pastors, elders, and deacons serving our Lord together.*
2. My desire is that God would have favor upon all of you and out of His grace, you would experience His deep abiding peace. This grace and peace flow from the heart of God the Father and the Lord Jesus Christ.[2]

Paul's Prayer and Love

3-4. Every time I think about you, I am thankful and in my daily prayers, I mention you to the Father with joy in my heart.

5. I pray, I am thankful, and I have joy in my heart for you because of your partnership with me in the Gospel of the Lord Jesus Christ. You responded to the Gospel when I first shared the Gospel with you and your trust in Christ has lasted even until now.

The Certainty of God's Working in Our Lives

6. I am confident that God has started a work in your life through *being born again*, and He will continue this work until you *arrive in Heaven* with Jesus. *Nothing will prevent you from being Christ-like.*[3]

Philippians—The Path to Joy!

7. I am correct in thinking this way of you because I love you and *the evidence is in the fact* that we are partners together in suffering, as I am in prison and you are a defense and confirmation of the Gospel. *[You are a defense because you heard the Gospel, you believed it, you are proclaiming it, and you are in submission to it as you live your daily lives. Living the Gospel allows others to see what the Gospel does in real time and real life.]* This is all by God's unearned favor upon you.[4]
8. God is my witness that I so desire to see you and I have such great love for you as Jesus Christ Himself does. My tender love for you is an expression of how much Jesus Christ loves you.[5]

Love Increases as We Grow in God's Word

9. And this I am praying that your love will increase abundantly as you grow deeper in your knowledge and understanding *of God's Word*.[6]
10. Then you will be able to approve, by investigating *the Word of God*, what is the best way to live your life with sincerity and without offense until you arrive in Heaven with Jesus.[7]
11. You have been filled with good works by Jesus Christ Himself, for the glory and praise of God, and these good works continue to flow through you into everyday life.[8]

Philippians—The Path to Joy!

Problems Have Purposes!

12. Now I want you to know that everything that has happened to me has had a purpose and that purpose has been to cause the Gospel to reach others.[9]
13. Indeed the Gospel has been furthered so much so that the whole palace knows along with everyone else that I am imprisoned because of my stand with Christ.
14. Also, many of the brothers in the Lord *Jesus Christ* have become confident to speak boldly about Him and the Gospel without fear because of my imprisonment.[10]
15. Granted, some are proclaiming Christ because of envy and strife, but others are proclaiming Christ because of good intentions.
16. The first group proclaims Christ with selfish reasons and wrong motives. *They are not sincerely preaching Christ for God's glory or for those who are lost.* They are attempting to add more trouble to my imprisonment.[11]
17. However, the others *are proclaiming Christ* out of love, knowing that I have been put here to provide answers for the Gospel.
18. What does it matter? At least with every means with wrong motives or right motives Jesus Christ is being preached. And in this, I rejoice about it and I will continue to rejoice that Christ is being preached.[12]
19. I will continue to rejoice because I know, I am certain, that this trial will turn out for my

Philippians—The Path to Joy!

deliverance; *in other words,* I will be so empowered by the Holy Spirit and your prayers *that I will not deny Christ, but stay strong in my position for Jesus Christ.*[13]

Strength to Stand Up for Christ

20. Actually, concerning my expectations and hope, I will not allow anyone to shame me for trusting in Jesus Christ, indeed with all of my openness about Jesus, in this same manner, Christ will be magnified by me now and forever whether through my life or my death.
21. Indeed, the thing that concerns me the most is if I live, I live for Christ, if I die, I am actually better off in Heaven with Jesus.
22. But if I am to go on living and not die, I will continue to work for Jesus and will see more results. What if I were able to choose between the two? I don't know which I would chose—life or death.
23. And the whole idea of wanting to live and serve the Lord or go and be with Him in heaven puts serious pressure on me. For the longing I am having to leave and be with Christ is so much more better than staying here on earth.[14]
24. But to stay here on earth is more important for you.
25. And convinced of this, I know that I will stay on earth, and continue with all of you for your progress and joy in the faith.

Philippians—The Path to Joy!

26. The result will be that your happiness and rejoicing will really increase in Jesus Christ with me because I will be with you again.
27. Stay living a life appropriate of the Gospel of Christ, that whether I come and see you or not, the things I want to hear about you are: that you are standing together as one spirit and soul struggling for the faith of the Gospel.[15]
28. And do not be afraid of anyone, certainly not by those who oppose you, their opposition to you and the Gospel is proof of their own destruction, but in regard to you, their opposition is proof of your salvation and that is from God.[16]
29. Because from God's perspective, He graciously gave you the opportunity for the sake of Christ not only to believe on Him, but to suffer for Him.[17]
30. You are having the same conflict that you saw me having, and now hear that I am still having the same conflict.

Philippians—The Path to Joy!

Chapter One Notes

[1] The wording in the Greek Text is overseers, but the meaning is clear that God is referring to all of the eldership in the church, which includes the overseers, pastors, and elders. You are to be walking under the authority of the eldership in the church; see Hebrews 13:17 and I Thessalonians 5:12. Being under authority in the church is very important for your personal growth. Keep in mind, however, that you should always study the Scriptures so you are able to evaluate what you are told and taught so that it coincides with the scriptures.

[2] Grace will always produce peace. If you are always tired and burnt out, then you need to consider if you are drawing from the grace of the Lord Jesus Christ. How do we get grace from God? 1. Prayer (Hebrews 4:16), 2. Word of God (Acts 20:32), 3. Humility (James 4: 6-10). Work on being humble before God so that He is willing to give you extra grace.

[3] God is going to do whatever it takes to conform you into the image of Christ. All of the hardships and all of the awful experiences you may have had are designed for a purpose. Nothing is wasted. Even the sins you have committed, God uses them for good for those who love God and are called according to His purpose (Romans 8:28-29). The key is to trust Jesus Christ to be responsible for you and to perform His work in you through the Holy Spirit.

[4] The Gospel will impact your life so that it changes you. This is regeneration or being born again. You receive the Holy Spirit at the moment of salvation, and He works in your life so that you change. If your life has not changed, you most likely are not converted to Christ. Make an honest assessment of your life to ensure you are born-again. On the other hand, if you are still sinning, don't be in despair because you will battle against sin until you arrive in

Philippians—The Path to Joy!

Heaven. It is the direction of your heart, not the perfection of your lifestyle. It is the characterization of your lifestyle. The concern I have is that people have been taught that if you say a "sinner's prayer" and ask Jesus into your heart that you are saved and going to heaven, but that is not correct. Salvation comes from trusting in Jesus Christ to be the payment for your sin debt against God.

This trust includes repentance from sin and a surrendering of your life to Jesus Christ. When you repent of your sin, you are forsaking all other gods and all other ways to Heaven and forsaking all sin. If you are not surrendered to Jesus Christ, take this time to cry out to God that He would forgive you through Jesus Christ and tell Him that you are trusting Jesus Christ right now. Tell God that you are surrendering to Christ.

[5] The love in our hearts for others is placed in our hearts by the Holy Spirit. This love is an indicator that Jesus loves that person as well. When we are loved by believers, it also indicates that Jesus is loving us.

[6] Biblical love grows in us in direct proportion to our study and understanding of God's Word. The Holy Spirit transforms our lives into the very image of Jesus Christ as we study and behold His glory in the Scriptures. As this takes place, you will grow in your love for God and for others. Therefore, you pray for your love to grow and you study His word and watch the Spirit of God transform you from the inside out. Be patient, however; it takes time to grow strong in the Lord Jesus. Keep working on your Christian life and yielding to Him.

[7] As you learn the Word of God, you will be able to approve the best way to live your life. You will make decision based upon facts and the truth of the Scriptures by using logic and reason. This will give you the grace to make sincere decisions that are not offensive

Philippians—The Path to Joy!

to God. You will find that your choices will override your emotions thereby making much better decisions. God desires for His people to make decisions based on the Word of God with logic and reason.

[8] Filled with good works is equal to being filled with righteous fruit. The good works have the quality of righteousness. They are pure works. The Greek grammar reveals that there is a point in time when Jesus fills the believer with righteous acts, and they continue to flow from the believer's life. As you are filled with the Holy Spirit, you will produce Christian character called the fruit of the Spirit: Love, Joy, Peace, Patience, Kindness, Goodness, Faithfulness, Meekness, and Self-control. Further, Jesus through His Spirit, will produce works that are characterized by righteousness that only He can produce in a believer. These works will glorify and praise God.

[9] Every bad thing that happens to you has a purpose behind it. Here Paul says his imprisonment has furthered the Gospel. God uses problems in our lives to advance the Gospel of Jesus Christ so others hear of Him. Trust Him to be using your hardships for His glory and your good. Everything God does is ultimately for His glory.

[10] Others are watching how you manage yourself during problems and your response is able to give others courage to go on in difficult times. In this case, others became courageous to preach the Gospel even though they would be persecuted.

[11] There are those who would want to cause you more problems in life. Be empowered by God's grace for Kingdom Living. Live the way our master taught us in the sermon on the mount in Matthew 5-7. You must forgive, look to Jesus, and walk by faith in His Word. Draw strength from His promises in the Word. Kingdom Living is Walking on the Path of Life. Staying on the Path of Life with enable you to

Philippians—The Path to Joy!

be on the Path of joy.

[12] Joy is the theme of the book of Philippians. The word joy is used in the book one way or another about 17 times. God wants us to rejoice in life. He wants us to rejoice even when life is difficult. We are to rejoice in Christ. Rejoicing is an act of the will. It is your attitude that counts. Feelings follow behavior. Therefore, by the act of your will, rejoice in Christ. If you will rely on the Holy Spirit, He will enable you to rejoice and if you ask Him to control your life, He will produce joy in your heart. Asking the Holy spirit to control you is yielding your life to Him. You must begin to live by faith on God's Word and act on the Bible. By the act of your will, choose to rejoice in Christ.

[13] Verse 19-20 are so important because Paul is saying that he will be delivered meaning that he will not turn his back on Christ during persecution. He says that because of their prayers and the supply of power by the Holy Spirit. he will not be ashamed of Christ. He will be strong. He must rely on the prayers of others and the Holy Spirit for power.

[14] Paul desired to go to Heaven so deeply that he had serious pressure on his heart about staying on earth or leaving. He was not suicidal. He just longed to be with the Lord and be out of his body. But he knew the church on earth needed him. They needed his teachings. They needed his courage and encouragement. They needed his prayers. Yes, sometimes you want to go to heaven, but your job is not finished yet. You are still here, and you have a work to do. Keep your eyes on the Lord Jesus. Ask the Holy Spirit for strength. You will get through your pain. It will be worth it all.

[15] God gives staying power to the believer so that you live your life appropriately as a believer in Christ, and that you are able to keep on fighting for the Gospel to get it into the hands of others. This is

Philippians—The Path to Joy!

the purpose of the believer: to stay strong in the Gospel of Christ and to share it with others. Having a definitive purpose helps keep you healthy. We have to work with other believers as one person, not divided.

[16] If you are being opposed because of the Gospel of Christ, then it reveals that you are a believer. But listen, if you are being opposed because of your manner in which you are presenting the Christian life, then that is on you. If others are persecuting you because of your faith, then it shows that they are fitted for destruction. According to the scriptures, there are those who are designed for destruction and will thereby reveal the great mercies of God on those who believe.

[17] The Word He graciously gave is one word in the Greek language and it has the combination grace with giving. Out of God's grace and purposes, He has chosen some to be persecuted for His sake. That is God's prerogative. If you are being persecuted, accept it. Trust Him to help you go through it. Do not turn your back on Jesus. His Holy Spirit will empower you. You cannot feel grace. His grace just powers you through your problems as you reach out to Jesus Christ for grace.

Philippians—The Path to Joy!

CHAPTER 2

Humility the Absolute in Christianity

1. Therefore, since there is encouragement, let it be found in Christ, since there is comfort let it be found with love, since there is fellowship, let it be found by the Holy Spirit, since there is such fellowship by the Holy Spirit, let it be found with feelings of affection and mercy.[1]
2. I am commanding you to fill me up completely with joy by thinking the same thoughts, having the same love, being as one person, thinking on the same purpose.[2] *[And what are those thoughts, what is that same love, what is it being like one person and what is the same purpose?]*
3. Do not do anything against each other that divides the church or is self-seeking glory, but with humility hold up each other above yourself.[3]
4. Do not just look out for your own selves, but also each of you consider the interest and needs of others.

Jesus is our Model for Humility!

5. I am commanding you to be actively entertaining in your mind even the same thoughts or attitude that was in Jesus Christ.[4]
6. Jesus Christ has been and is in the form of God and being equal with God He did not hold onto the glory as to display it.[5]
7. He emptied himself of His divine rights and glory in order to take on the role of a slave, to become a

Philippians—The Path to Joy!

human being, and when He came as a man in His body,[6]

8. He humbled Himself by becoming obedient even to the point of death, the death by the cross.[7]
9. And consequently, God exalted Him above all and gave Him the name above every name.[8]
10. That at the name of Jesus every knee will bow. Everyone and everything in Heaven, on earth, and under the earth will bow the knee to Jesus Christ.
11. And every person, everything, and in every language will openly acknowledge and declare that Jesus Christ is LORD to the glory of God the Father.

Work at your Christian Life

12. Therefore, my dear loved ones, as you have always obeyed, not in my presence only, but now in my absence, put much more work into your salvation to its very completion, *in other words, put greater emphasis on working fully at your Christian life,* with fear and trembling.[9]
13. For God is the One working in you to produce both the desire and power so that you are able to accomplish what brings Him pleasure.[10]
14. Do everything without complaining and/or arguing.[11]
15. This way your conduct will be once and for all—Blameless and your motive will be having Proper Intentions—Being children of God without needing to be rebuked among a generation of people who have wandered from God's intention and purpose who also have become perverted. Among them you

Philippians—The Path to Joy!

are shining as lights in the world.[12]

16. You are holding onto the Word of life and this is cause for my rejoicing in the day of Christ that I have not lived or worked in vain.[13]

Three Biblical Models for you to Follow

17. Yes, if also, I am *offering myself* to be poured out as a drink offering upon the sacrifice and public service for your faith. I am rejoicing and rejoice with all of you.[14]
18. Further, in the very same way I am rejoicing, I want all of you to rise to the same level of rejoicing with me![15]
19. *By the Lord Jesus's will* I expect to send Timothy to you soon that I may also be comforted when I know how all of you are doing.[16]
20. Because I have no one else like Timothy, he has the same spirit as mine, who truly cares for your wellbeing.
21. Everyone else is looking out for themselves and not that of the interest of Jesus Christ.[17]
22. But you know that he has proven to be trusted, because he has served with me, as a child does with his father, for the purpose of spreading the Gospel.[18]
23. Therefore, I expect to send him as soon as I know how things are going to go with me *in this situation.*
24. But I am convinced that with the Lord's help I will also quickly be coming to you.
25. Also, I considered it necessary to send Epaphroditus back to you, my brother, fellow-laborer, and solider,

Philippians—The Path to Joy!

but your messenger and minister sent to meet my need.
26. I am sending him back because he strongly desired to see all of you and was being distressed because you heard that he was sick.
27. For indeed he was sick. He almost died. But God had mercy on him, moreover, God not only had mercy on him, but on me as well. Lest I would be experiencing sorrow upon sorrow.[19]
28. Therefore, I sent him promptly that once more you may rejoice knowing that he is well, and I am less sad.
29. So, receive him in the Lord with joyfulness and hold him and others like him in high regard giving them respect.[20]
30. Because he almost died for the work of Christ, risking his life to do for me what you could not do for me.

Philippians—The Path to Joy!

Chapter Two Notes

---

[1] These are conditional statements, and most all translations take the apodosis as verse 2; however, verse 1 and verse 2 should be taken as individual sentences. Verse 1 has the apodosis for each protases. Further, each apodosis should read as either a declarative or imperative. It is preferably an imperative. Therefore, they are taken as a command. God is not assuming this church already has these behaviors; He is commanding them to find their encouragement in Jesus Christ. There comfort is to be found in love. This would be love for Christ and also love for each other. They are to be choosing to love each other. It is the Greek word agape for love, and it is love by choice not unconditional love. It is obedience to God's Word by choosing to love one another with the sixteen beautiful qualities as outlined in I Corinthians 13. It would behoove you to study those sixteen qualities to discover what love does. Take one quality a month and spend 30 days saturating your mind in one, then go on to the next one for the next month. This would take you about 16 months, but by the time you were done studying them, you would be growing in love.

How to study each one for the month: 1. Learn a definition for the quality that you are studying. 2. Memorize the definition. 3. Look up a thought about the quality for every day of the month. 4. Put them on the calendar. This would be your seed thought for the day, then every day, look at the calendar and take the seed thought with you throughout the day. 5. Each day look up 2-5 articles about the quality you are studying. 6. Write down one thought you learned from the articles. 7. Share that thought with someone during the day. Do this every day. Is this a lot of work? Yes, but if you are serious about growing in Christ and as a person, you must put the time into it.

Philippians—The Path to Joy!

² When Paul uses the term for fill me up, it is a term that means to be filled up to the brim. He wants them to provide a basis for his joy, but how? The answer is not in verse 2, but it is in verse 3. In verse 2, he says to have the same thoughts, about what? The same love, but how? Being of the same soul or be one, but what about? Having the same purpose, but what is the purpose? The answer is found in verse 3—it is to be humble. Humility is the number one character quality that each believer in Christ is to have in their lives. But it takes work at being humble. He will explain what it is, but for now, you must know that if you are in recovery or you want to change your life in any part of your life, you will have to put on humility. If you want to be a true Christian, you must be humble.

Another important note is that Paul is not saying it was their responsibility to make him happy. The point God is communicating to each of us is that Christian joy is derived from being humble before God. God the Father is commanding all of us to have the same thoughts about humility, the same love grounded in humility, be as one person centered around humility, having the same purpose with humility being the target as a body in Christ. This fills up the Father's heart with joy when He sees His people living with humility. You cannot encounter Jesus Christ without being humble. Pride keeps you from Jesus. But as they put on humility and were acting like Christ, this gave Paul a basis for him to be completely filled up with Joy.

³ This is the opposite of what the world says. The world promotes putting yourself first. This leads to anger and unhappiness. True humility drives us to put others first, and it is a paradox, but we find joy in our own lives by truly loving others and helping them in their needs. I understand if you are unhealthy and co-dependent, this will lead you to anger and unhappiness. Therefore, the emphasis is on true humility.

Philippians—The Path to Joy!

⁴ What were the thoughts and/or attitudes? He will explain, but it goes back to the previous verse—humility. Paul is now getting ready to show you what humility looks like. Jesus modeled humility so there would be clarity. The Greek word used for thoughts or attitude is a word that means thinking. Thinking is vital to changing your life. If you change the way you think, you will change your life. In this case, it is having the same mindset that Jesus had. How do you get that mindset? You must study the Bible intently. You must be renewing your mind. Saturating your mind in the Scriptures. The daily verse sent to you is not ample to change your life.

⁵ The word form means that Jesus Christ has the very nature of God. It is in the present tense in the Greek, and means he is and has always existed in the form of God. This verse is difficult to translate and with all of the various translations, it seems to be more confusing. But the meaning is that Jesus Christ was and is God. God Himself is Spirit and you cannot see God. Jesus has the nature of God and He was/is equal to God, but He did not come to earth to display His glory in His first advent. God explains in the following verses the intent and purpose of His coming the first time. It is to be clear that Jesus Christ came the first time to offer His body as a sacrifice and payment for all of those who would believe in Him as their Lord. The second advent of Christ will be displaying Him in all of His glory, but not the first advent. Therefore, our Lord was willing to lay aside His glory for now. He was humble. He modeled for you. You do not have to chase after your own glory, nor do you have to chase after your selfish interests. You are here for Christ and His purpose for your life. Serve Him. Be caught up in the Wonder of His Glory that are all throughout the Scriptures.

⁶ Jesus empties Himself is the Theology of Kenosis. Christ emptied Himself, but of what did He empty Himself? Some say of His deity. But His deity is His nature. He has never stopped being God. He

Philippians—The Path to Joy!

always was and always will be God. When He took on a human body, He became the God-man. He is both God and man, and will ever be so. Jesus has two natures, but they are intertwined and cannot be separated. He emptied Himself of the rights and privileges of being God. He did not display His glory and did not make a spectacular coming into the world the first time. The second coming will be different.

[7] He was obedient to the Father. He modeled obedience. You too are to be obedient to God. Jesus gave up His rights. He gave up His rights to His own will. He gave up His rights to His own way. This is a picture of true Christianity. If you are living for your own purposes and desires, you are not living the Christian life. There is a great possibility that you are not a true born-again Christian. Luke 9:23 gives us the way of the true Christian. Luke 9:23 says, [23] And he said to *them* all, "If any *man* will come after me, let him deny himself, and take up his cross daily, and follow me." This is not just discipleship. It is Biblical salvation. A saved person is a disciple. No discipleship, not Christianity.

[8] Verses 9-11 are very important. Please read carefully so that you understand what God is saying and what He means by what He says. This is the goal from eternity past that Christ would be exalted among the nations as the God of the universe and that His people whom God had chosen before the foundation of the world would praise the glory of Christ forever. All people will exalt and glorify Jesus Christ by publicly acknowledging that He is the LORD. Everyone will bow to Jesus Christ in the end. The believers will do it gladly. Unbelievers will do it, but not gladly. All of those who reject Christ are fitted for destruction and will glorify Him forever by paying their sin debt that they owe to the Creator in a place called the lake of fire. God is willing to accept the payment in hell for all eternity by anyone who desires to pay their own debt rather than receive Jesus Christ as Lord and accept the payment He provided

Philippians—The Path to Joy!

on the cross. Either way, someone has to pay for your sin. Either it will be you or Jesus. The choice is yours. If you want Him, then cry out to Jesus Christ right now for forgiveness and His righteousness for your life. Do not delay so it does not get too late that you cannot respond to Him.

[9] Verse 12 is not saying that you should or could work for your salvation. You cannot work for salvation. If you add anything on to what the Lord Jesus Christ has done, you will go to hell. Jesus plus anything sends people to hell, but Jesus alone saves His people from their sins. God is actually telling you to work at your Christian Life. The word work means to labor at it. It actually means work to the point of exhaustion until the job is complete. You have to put effort into the Christian Life. You have to keep working at it until it is finished. Don't stop working at your Christian life. Many people seem to think that God will just do the work for them. I have had many people say God is not answering their prayers to take away a sinful habit or to change their life in an area. God has not set it up where all we have to do is pray about it and it "magically" goes away. It is hard work to overcome sinful habits. You have to put the effort into it. Not that you are alone in the process. Our Lord will enable you by the Person and Power of the Holy Spirit. But you have to put the work into it. Read II Peter 1: 5-11.

[10] God works in your life through the Holy Spirit. Your responsibility is to be filled or controlled by the Holy Spirit. You will read this throughout the JEN Translation. Yield your life to the Holy Spirit. Be empowered by Him. Ask Him to control. Fill yourself with His Word so that you are able to yield to Him. Let the Word of Christ saturate you.

[11] Arguing and complaining is an indicator that you are not filled with the Spirit. It is an indicator that you are not walking in Wisdom. Learn to control your tongue and attitude so that you do

Philippians—The Path to Joy!

not complain or argue with others. Arguing and complaining are the works of the flesh. It is what non-believers do. You trust God. You rejoice in Christ by faith. You believe in the Sovereign work of God on your behalf. Know that He is working, guiding, and leading you.

[12] The once and for all statement is used because the verb, γίνομαι, is in the aorist and provides a basis for the idea to be a permanent standing of blamelessness and purity of heart. Their conduct has no offenses and their motives are not mixed with self-interest. The point is that the present generation of the unsaved world has not damaged them in conduct or motive. This is the objective: you must keep yourself from getting damaged by the present world. Guard your conduct. Guard your motives and keep your eyes and heart on the Lord Jesus Christ.

[13] Holding onto is the Greek word for holding forth or retaining. Some translate "holding onto" as "holding out" in regards to preaching, but it does not mean to preach the Word. The Greek word zoe, which means life is in the genitive, giving the Word a qualitative aspect. This means that the Word is life. The Word is allowing these Christians to be lights in the world. It was not their quality of life because in this passage Paul was admonishing them to be blameless and pure. The emphasis in the Christian life is that we are to be the salt of the earth and light in the world. It is the Christian "holding onto" the Word of life, and the Word is illuminating through the Christian. It is the Word that brings conviction to sin and shows light unto the path for others to see. This is done through the Person of the Holy Spirit as He takes the Word of Life that we hold onto and exposes it to others. The Word of Life gives us life through the Holy Spirit. But, with all of this said, it does not mean your life is not important because it is highly important how you live. Verses 12-13 teach that you are to be obedient to God. Your responsibility is to continue studying the

Philippians—The Path to Joy!

Word, trust it, be in submission to it, and share it with others, then those around you will see the light.

[14] The verb poured out is taken as a middle voice rather than passive as most translations take it. This is due to the fact that who is the one giving his life for the service of God? God is not doing this (God is not making him), and the Roman government is not giving Paul's life or taking it. Paul has given his life and thereby, will die for the service of God so that others would be saved. It is middle not passive in voice. If you are to serve the LORD, it will cost you time, energy, money, and maybe even your life. However, we only have one life to live and only what is done for Christ is of eternal significance. You ought to consider devoting your life to Christ in service for Him. Jim Elliot has said, "He is no fool who gives what he cannot keep to gain that which he cannot lose." You cannot keep your life so you might as well give it to God so you will not lose it. The drink offering to the Jews symbolized the voluntary surrender of everything to God.

[15] This verse is taken in an adverbial sense and not tautology. Paul is not repeating verse 17 in a different way. He is wanting them to rise to the same level of rejoicing with him that he is rejoicing. They must have been sad due to Paul's circumstances and he wanted them to be rejoicing about it because they have faith in Christ because of his life service and even his death if need be. I want to remind you that rejoicing is by the act of your will. You have to rejoice by choice. You can do this even in the most difficult situations. You are not to go by your feelings even though you don't feel happy and your feelings are sad, depressed, or filled full of anxieties. By faith, you rejoice in Christ. It is not wrong to act against your feelings. Your feelings are to bow to the Scriptures. Some people think it is a lie to act positive when they have negative feelings. That is far from the truth. You are to act according to what the Bible says no matter how you feel.

Philippians—The Path to Joy!

¹⁶ Originally, I wanted this verse to state, "I expect the Lord Jesus to send Timothy" because Paul says he will send Timothy "in Jesus Christ." The word "in" is the Greek word "en" and in this case, it is used as an instrumental, meaning that it is "by" Jesus that Paul will send Timothy. In other words, if it is the will of Jesus, Paul will send Timothy. So in reality, this means that Jesus will send Timothy, and Jesus will use Paul to send Timothy. This is how life is. God will accomplish His will and purposes and will use people to do His will. So in reality, it is God doing the work through people. God will use you as well. You should be available to Him. Also, I think it is important to say that you should be looking to God each moment to know what His will is and to acknowledge that you will do something if it is God's will. Do not be presumptuous. The Latin term is Deo Volente—God willing!! Always keep this in mind that you will only get to do what God wills to be done.

¹⁷ Paul's point is that Timothy is the only one that is exclusive of all other things and is totally devoted to that of the purposes of Jesus Christ. The others still had interest of Christ but were involved in their own lives as well. This is not a condemnation but rather a fact. Paul needed someone who would be devoted to the things of Christ and not get distracted because of family or business needs. If anyone has no interest in the things of Jesus Christ, then they are not true born-again Christians. Please don't be deceived: if you have no desire to read the Bible, go to church, pray, and such spiritual disciplines; you must then realize that the percentage is very high for you to be unsaved even if you prayed a prayer and ask Jesus in your heart. It is not the prayer that saves, but it is active trust in Christ for the payment of your sin debt against God. Please examine yourself to see if you are in the faith.

¹⁸ Timothy's character has been tried and proven to be trustworthy. He was the real deal. He was absolutely devoted to Jesus Christ and to people so that they would be saved and would grow in their

Philippians—The Path to Joy!

faith. Timothy invested in eternity for God's glory and praise. This is what should be motivating us to give our life for eternity—God's glory and the praise of His glory for all eternity. It is so Jesus will be honored for all eternity.

[19] Would be experiencing is the Greek word ἔχω in the aorist tense, which is an ingressive meaning that Paul would have entered into a state of being sad: sadness about his sickness, sadness about his death, sadness about losing his assistance, sadness for the people back at his church. But the question is, how can Paul be desiring these folks to be joyful one minute, then telling them he would have gone into a state of grief with sadness upon sadness? Is this a contradiction? Not at all!! The believer in Christ is able to rejoice by the act of the will and enter into a state of sadness. The heart remains joyful and peaceful because of the position of being in Christ. You have to keep your mindset and attitude on the Hope that is in Jesus Christ. It is the future you looked at. You are a pilgrim just passing through this world on to the next world. What takes you beyond suffering, beyond pain, beyond sadness, is the desire for Christ, a desire for His righteousness, a desire for His holiness. The more you desire Him and seek after Him, you will lose sight of the immediate pain and suffering.

[20] It is important to give respect to those who give their life in service for Jesus Christ. You do not see much respect given in the era that we live in, but it is important for you as a true believer to follow the admonition of the Lord to give respect and honor to our leaders, parents, pastors, elders, elderly, and such. You are to respect the office of these. Respecting and honoring others does not mean you agree with everything they do, and it certainly does not mean you permit them to abuse you. However, it does mean that you honor them even if you have to disagree with them. If you disagree with them, the disagreement is not to be based upon opinions, but on the Word of God. You should have chapter and

Philippians—The Path to Joy!

verse of what you disagree with them. In the era in which we live, almost all disagreements are based upon opinions. If this is the case, then you have to yield your opinion to the leaders: parents, pastors, elders, elderly, and such. Why do you have to yield your opinion to them? Because God has placed them over you. Once again, I am not talking about any kind of abuse. Abuse of any sort—spiritual, physical, sexual, emotional, and such—are all sinful and violate the Word of God. The Word of God is always our default for knowing right and wrong and if it is an opinion or not. If it is not in the Bible, it is an opinion.

Philippians—The Path to Joy!

CHAPTER 3

Warning Against Deceivers

1. As to the rest of what I want to say, my brothers, rejoice in the Lord. Writing the same things to you is not any trouble for me and to you it is security.[1]
2. Watch out for the dogs, watch out for the evil workers, watch out for the mutilators.[2]
3. For we are the true circumcised who, by the Spirit of God, are worshipping and boasting in Christ Jesus and not having any confidence in the flesh to save.[3]

Warning against Self-Righteousness

4. And if it were possible to provide enough good works to save oneself, if these others think they could, I could more than they could.
5. Because I was circumcised the eighth day, born of the nation Israel, of the tribe of Benjamin, a true Hebrew, according to the law, a Pharisee.[4]
6. As far as my passion for the law, I persecuted the church, I lived according to the law perfectly without any fault.

Christ is Our Righteousness

7. However, the very things that were so important and I thought were an advantage to me I have counted as worthless because of Christ.[5]
8. But even more so, I count all of these things to be a loss because of the superiority of the knowledge of

Philippians—The Path to Joy!

Christ Jesus My Lord. Because of Him I have disregarded everything, and I count all of my good works as worthless so that I could have Christ,[6]

9. and be found in Him, not having my own righteousness by following the law perfectly, but that which comes through faith in Christ, the righteousness that is imputed from God on the basis of faith.

Christ is Our Goal

10. I now truly know Him, and the Power of His resurrection and the partnership of His sufferings being conformed to His death.
11. And for certain, one way or another, I will be in the resurrection from the dead.[7]
12. Not that I had already obtained or have already been perfected. I am continuing my pursuit of perfection and with certainty, I will get what I am pursuing, since I was pursued and captured by Christ.[8]
13. Brothers! I am not considering myself as having obtain the completion of the death of Christ, but this one thing, I am forgetting the things that are behind me and I am stretching forward,
14. after the goal I am pursuing which is the prize of high calling of God in Christ Jesus.[9]

Walk in Unity

15. Likewise, then, all of us who are mature keep thinking on the things I have said. And if there are

Philippians—The Path to Joy!

some of you who are thinking different than what I said, eventually God will help you to understand.

16. Moreover, concerning all that we have attained, keep living by that same standard and keep thinking the same thoughts.[10]
17. Brothers! Follow my life as a pattern for living and consider those who are following our model for living.[11]
18. For many, of whom, I often told you and now while weeping I am telling you, live as the enemies of the cross of Christ.[12]
19. Whose destiny is destruction, whose god is their stomach, and whose boasting is in their disgraceful behavior, these are the ones who entertain worldly thinking.[13]
20. For our citizenship exist in Heaven, and it is from Heaven that we are fully expecting the Lord and Savior Jesus Christ to return.[14]
21. Who will transform our lowly body so that it will be conformed to His glorious body by the same ability and power that He has to cause all things to be in submission to Himself.[15]

Philippians—The Path to Joy!

Chapter Three Notes

[1] It is security for Paul to remind them to rejoice. This is a safety net. It is protection in the Christine life.

[2] The three terms Paul uses in this verse all refer to the same people. They are dogs, evil workers, and mutilators. Why? They are teaching false doctrine. They are leading people away from Jesus and leading people straight to hell. They are dogs meaning they are unclean and filthy, also, they are vicious and dangerous. However, they do not come into the church looking vicious. They look appealing. They look successful. They are subtle. You cannot tell them apart from others except for their teachings, at least, at first. They are evil workers. They put a lot of time, energy, and money into reaching people with their false teachings. But the work itself is evil. It is deceptive work. Finally, they mutilate. This refers to Jewish circumcision. They imposed the Old Testament law on people to place works for salvation. If anyone adds anything to Jesus, it equals damnation. Jesus plus nothing equals salvation. Jesus plus anything equals eternity spent in hell. An example would be baptism. Baptism does not save, but there are those who say you have to be baptized to be forgiven of your sins. Baptism is an outward expression of your faith in Christ, but it is not to be saved. If you trust baptism to save you, you will go to hell. Solus Christus—Christ alone! Christ is the only way.

[3] This is a difficult verse to understand because of how to translate the word Spirit in the dative. There are those who say that the Spirit is the object of worship in this passage, but it seems that this would not be fitting in context of the discussion Paul is having in chapter 2 and 3. It is better to take the word Spirit as instrumental dative meaning; that it is by the Holy Spirit that God is to be worshiped. In context, it appears that Christ Jesus is the object of worship and boasting. Our salvation, glory, and worship are all in Christ. He is the mediator. In the sense the Godhead, Father, Son,

Philippians—The Path to Joy!

and Holy Spirit are God—Three in One--are to be honored and worshiped, we are directed to be Christo Centric. Christ Centered! This is the idea in context of the book. We are told in John 16 that the Holy Spirit would glorify Jesus, so it does not seem reasonable in this passage. Paul is saying to worship the Holy Spirit. What Paul is driving home in the hearts of the reader is that true salvation is not of any kind of works. It is all of God. Those who truly believe in Jesus as their Lord and Savior have a new heart, and they have the Holy Spirit placed in them to fill them and guide them into worship and service to Jesus Christ. This is all accomplished by Jesus Christ, so you boast in Him. You praise Him. You serve and worship Him for what He has done for you. This is the path to joy. This is the way of the Christian life.

4 The Jewish Nation was handpicked by God to be His chosen people. However, it still took and even now takes personal faith in Christ to be saved. But the Jewish nation missed that point. They thought that the way to God was to be born a Jew. If you were born a Jew, they thought you had a special place with God. They further believed that all others were rejected by God. This is the reason Paul is discussing in verses 4-6 his National Heritage. He now knows that he was wrong, and it is not about your nationality, but rather about what you believe about Jesus Christ. It is all about Christ, not about you. Therefore, he is letting all of his former beliefs and ideas go. He is embracing God's way of salvation. Don't hold on to the past. God never asks you did you believe at some time in the past. His Word always refers to the present. Are you, right now, believing in Jesus Christ for the forgiveness of your personal sins? That is the point. That is the question. One further thought, if you are coming to Christ just so your life gets better, then that is idolatry. You will not get saved just to better your life. You get saved because your sins are hideous before a Holy God, and you will go to hell without receiving God's sacrifice for your

Philippians—The Path to Joy!

personal sins. There is only one way to God, and it is His way---Jesus Christ is the way, the truth, and the life (John 14:6).

[5] Works to earn salvation are detrimental. Paul had been relying on his heritage, good works, and the law to get approval from God. He worked hard at his perfection, but then when God opened His eyes to see that all of his good works missed the mark of God's glory, he placed his trust in Christ alone. When all of your good works are calculated, it is not enough to accumulate God's righteousness. There is only one way for you to be righteous before God. He must impute righteousness to you. He will only do that if you place your faith, hope, and trust in Jesus Christ for the forgiveness of your sins. It is Christ alone that saves. Jesus has completed the only work that satisfies the wrath of God. It was the death of Christ on the cross that made the acceptable payment for the sin of the believer. Try as you may, but you will always fall short. You must rest in Christ. Trust Him that He will save and keep you. You don't have to work to keep salvation either. You will always disappoint yourself. You will sin. You will not live up to your standards, nor God's, but you don't have to live up to it. Jesus has done it for you. Go out and love Him and serve Him, but keep trusting in the Gospel to save you. You need the Gospel every day.

[6] The loss of Paul's good works, the knowing of Christ, and being found in Him is a completed action. Paul is not saying he has to pursue this superior knowledge in Christ. He is not saying he has to pursue to be found in Christ. He knows Christ. He is found in Christ. He belongs to Christ. He has let go of all of his stuff for Christ. Now he is being conformed into the death of Christ. Knowing Jesus Christ as Lord is superior to any and all other good works. The knowledge of Christ is not comparable to any other way to God. All other ways fall short and leave the person in his sins. In the final judgement, the person still in his sins will make his own sacrifice for

Philippians—The Path to Joy!

sins thereby spending eternity in the lake of fire paying off his sin debt.

However, it will take an eternity to satisfy the wrath of God because of His Holiness. Once Paul understood who Jesus Christ was and what He did in making the payment of sin by dying on the cross, Paul gladly disregarded everything he had done in order to have Christ Jesus the Lord as his sin bearer. You can have Jesus Christ as the payment for your sin too, if you would trust Him to forgive you, repent of your sins, and surrender to Him as your Lord. It is all by faith and not of yourself. Let go of everything and embrace Jesus Christ as your Lord. Call out to Him to save you and forgive you of your sin. This is your greatest need. Do not take a chance and think you are saved because of a time in your past that you have prayed a prayer and ask Jesus into your heart. Be sure now. That is my admonition to you.

[7] The Greek construction εἴ πως with the subjunctive provides the reader with the understanding that Paul is not questioning his resurrection. He is certain that it will happen. The uncertainty is in the means of his death. Will he die an old man, or will he die a martyr's death? He did not know, but he knew he would be resurrected from the dead regardless of how he dies.

If you know the Lord Jesus, you too will be resurrected from the dead. Keep your eyes on the hope in Christ and finish your earthly assignment. Paul is saying once he is resurrected then he will have finally attained perfection. He will be totally conformed into the image of Christ. He wants to be like Christ. He desires this so badly that he is longing for the day of his own resurrection from the dead to be conformed into the likeness of Christ.

[8] Paul is going back to verses 8-10 where he discusses that he let go of his good works, he is now found in Christ, he now knows Christ

Philippians—The Path to Joy!

and is being conformed into the death of Christ. This conforming to His death is the process of sanctification, dying to oneself. Deny yourself and live completely for Jesus Christ. It is surrendering your life to Christ and accepting His plan in your life without you fighting it. It is yielding to the Holy Spirit and working out your salvation as God works in you to manifest the very character of Christ.

"God is most glorified in you when Christ is most exemplified through you" [JEN]. Paul is saying that by letting go of all that he was doing with his life, such as following the law completely, being found in Him, and knowing Christ Jesus the Lord, has been a completed action. But being conformed into His death is a continuous experience. He has not obtained to it. He is not perfected or matured completely. He is still working on this aspect of his life.

The word perfected is the Greek word τελειόω. It means to be completed. In a practical standpoint, maturity would be used, but maturity does not quite give the meaning. It really does mean to be complete or finished. Paul is saying that he has not arrived at being conformed into the likeness of the death of Christ. This is not a completed action. He is still in pursuit of it, and it will not be accumulated until his death and he is in that resurrection. However, he is in pursuit of it. The verse further explains to you that your growth, your perfection, your being conformed into the image and likeness of Christ is based upon the fact that Christ captured you.

Christ pursued you, found you, and placed you in His body. Now you will be conformed into His death, but you are to pursue this conformity. It is, perhaps, a paradox. You are captured, and you pursue conformity until you capture it. If you know the Lord, you can be certain you will obtain it. It will be a reality so keep pursuing.

Philippians—The Path to Joy!

[9]In verses 13-14 Paul wants the church to clearly understand several points:

1). He has not arrived. He did not want them to get the idea that you would be able to arrive at perfection in this life.

2). You have to let go of your past. This includes the good and positive accomplishments as well as the bad and negative behaviors you have done. If you live in the past, you will hinder yourself from following after Jesus and holiness. Past achievements have the potential of causing you to be proud, to hang on to the past, to compare the present with the past. The past is the past. Leave it. You have past failures. You cannot change the past. You are to learn from those failures. You should see your failures in light of God's view from Scriptures. Learn the life lessons. Accept your failures and take courage to move forward by the power of the Holy Spirit. Forgetting things obviously does not mean you don't remember them. Paul was remembering them. It means you don't give them permission to affect you. You take responsibility for your actions, learn from it, and press on to what God is doing in your life. God is Sovereign, He allowed you to fail for a reason. Learn it, and go forward.

3). You stretch forward for the goal. What is the goal? What is the prize of the high calling of God? One thing for sure it is being conformed into the death of Christ. That is what Paul has been talking about. Being conformed into His death is dying to self. It is going from one suffering event to the next. It is becoming like Jesus. It is understanding Him more through the Scriptures. It is growing in love with Him more. It is reaching forward in growth as a believer in Christ. It is sanctification, being made holy by the Holy Spirit. Do you ever reach perfection? Not here, but in the resurrection you will.

Philippians—The Path to Joy!

[10] In verse 16, Paul is driving home one more point in their minds. They must keep living by the same rule that they have attained. The word rule in the Textus Receptus is the Greek word κανών, which is canon. It is the rule we are to live by and not deviate from it. What Paul is saying is that they must use the same measuring rod that they have been using for their Christian life. He is actually saying don't deviate from any point. The Greek word στοιχέω is an infinitive and used as an imperative. Paul is commanding you to keep in line. He is saying keep in step with each and every point. If you stop growing and reaching forward, you will go backwards. You never arrive in this world. It is possible to mature and lose your Christian maturity by not continuously living by the same standard. However, in order to do this, you have to keep reaching for the goal. You have to keep working out your salvation (2:12). You must keep working at your Christian life.

[11] Many people say they desire an example to follow for Christian living. Paul is saying follow the pattern he set forth. Live like he lived. Further, he says consider others who are living like he modeled. You have Paul and you have all of those around you who are following the pattern of the apostle Paul. Live the way they are living.

[12] The Bible says there are those who are fitted for destruction. They are the enemies of the cross. They serve themselves. They hate authority. They live for what they want. They are disobedient to God and His Word. Life centers about them. Do not be deceived if you are living for yourself, you cannot be a born-again Christian. You will go to hell if you do not repent. You say, "What if I prayed and asked Jesus into my heart?" "Will I still go to hell?" The answer is, of course you may, if you do not believe in Jesus Christ as the Lord of your life. True salvation is believing in Christ so that you are in submission to His will through the Word of God. It does not mean you are sinless or perfect, but you are striving to follow His

Philippians—The Path to Joy!

Word and you repent when you sin. We should be living in daily repentance.

[13] Change your thinking and you will change your life. This is why God says when you become a born-again Christian you are to renew your mind. Romans 12:2 says, "And be not conformed to this world: but be transformed by the renewing of your mind, that you may prove what is that good, and acceptable, and perfect, will of God." As a Christian, as you renew your mind, you will get a biblical worldview. However, if you do not renew your mind in the Word of God you will live as an atheist. The Bible will provide a basis for your knowledge and understanding of God. Your understanding of His attributes will determine how you live your life. Make sure your understanding of God is from the Scriptures, both the Old Testament and the New Testament.

[14] As Jesus was getting ready to ascend back into Heaven, He promised His disciples that He would return. In John 14, He said that He was preparing a place for His disciples in Heaven and He will come back for His people. You are to live as ambassadors of your true homeland—Heaven. You are to represent the True and Living God on this planet. Your expectation should be on Him and always looking for His return. He promised to return, and He will. Keep your eyes on the Lord Jesus. Stay focused on your purpose for being on earth.

[15] In the era of Paul, there were those who did not believe the body would be resurrected. Paul is saying in this passage that he is reaching for the resurrection of the dead. This was his goal to have a new body, and as he says in this verse, his resurrected body will be conformed into the same manner as the glorious resurrected body of Christ. His body will shine like the sun, but our bodies will shine like the stars. God has the ability to bring everybody back together again and conform it into a new state. This is the same

Philippians—The Path to Joy!

power that He will cause all people to be in submission to Him. His power is omnipotent. He has demonstrated His power already, but there is coming a time when He will demonstrate His power in an extreme manner that all people will know He is God. He is the true and living God that has expressed Himself through the person of the Lord Jesus Christ. Now is the time to be in complete submission to Him. Study His Word, walk in its authority over you, and live for His glory.

Philippians—The Path to Joy!

CHAPTER 4

Rejoice in the Lord Jesus

1. Therefore, my brothers, dear loved ones and the ones I long for, my joy and crown, even so dear loved ones keep standing firm in the Lord.[1]
2. I encourage Euodia and I encourage Syntyche to think the same thoughts in the Lord.[2]
3. Yes, I also request of you sincere Syzygus assist them who labored with me and Clement and the rest of my co-laborers for the Gospel whose names are in the book of life.
4. Always be happy in the Lord once more I will echo—be happy![3]
5. Make sure your yieldingness is known to all men, because the Lord is near.[4]

Do Not Worry About Anything

6. Do not be anxious about one thing, but in everything by your worship, and your supplication, with thanksgiving make your requests known to God.[5]
7. And the peace of God, *which* is greater than the whole mind, *His peace* will guard your hearts and your thoughts and *your perceptions* in Christ Jesus.[6]
8. Brothers, in conclusion I want to say, whatever is true, whatever is honorable, whatever is right, whatever is pure, whatever is lovable, whatever is commendable, continuously take inventory of everything that is excellent and worthy of praise.[7]

Philippians—The Path to Joy!

9. Also, what you learned and received and *what* you heard and saw me doing these same things *continuously* practice *in your life*, and the God of peace will be with you.[8]

Our Sufficiency is in Christ

10. I greatly rejoiced in the Lord that even now once again that you have revived your thinking of me indeed you were thinking of me all of this time, but you had no opportunity to do anything about it.
11. I am not telling you this because I have a need since I have learned to exist with contentment in whatever the circumstances.[9]
12. I know how to live both with nothing and I know how to live with an abundance, *actually* in every and all things I have been initiated into a lifestyle of living whether indeed I am completely satisfied or completely empty, having both more than I need and not having anything I need.[10]
13. I can do all things through Him empowering me.[11]
14. Yet you really did good in becoming a partner in my problems.[12]
15. But also, you know Philippians, that at the beginning of the Gospel when I departed from Macedonia, in regard to giving and receiving, not one church shared with me except only you.[13]
16. And concerning *your giving when I was* in Thessalonica *more than* once you sent to *supply* my need.

Philippians—The Path to Joy!

17. Not that I seek the gift, but in regard to you I seek that your fruit multiplies.[14]
18. Now I have everything I need, I even abound, *actually,* I am being filled *since having* received from Epaphroditus the gifts from you, a sweet-smelling fragrance, an acceptable sacrifice *that is* well pleasing to God.
19. Moreover, my God will completely fill your every need according to His wealth in glory through Christ.[15]

The Doxology

20. Now to our God and Father *be* the glory for all ages through eternity, Amen![16]

The Conclusion

21. Salute every saint in Christ Jesus, the brothers with me salute you.[17]
22. All of the saints salute you, especially those of Caesar's household.
23. The grace of the Lord Jesus Christ be among all of you.[18]

Philippians—The Path to Joy!

Chapter Four Notes

[1] This verse is packed full of love and affection that Paul has for the church at Philippi. God loves the church. Likewise, you should love the church. The church is not perfect by any means, but your love and affection for the church is an outward expression of the love that Jesus has for His people. The church belongs to God. Jesus purchased the church by His own death upon the cross. The pastors and elders are to be stewards over the church. They are to care for the church in His place and until He returns for the church. The church is to be a good ambassador for Christ while waiting for Him. The church is to be submissive to the pastors and elders of the church. They are to walk in unity and one accord. The church is not to be fighting or backbiting one another, nor are they to be usurping the authority of the pastors and elders. It is not about anyone's opinions. It is about studying the Sacred Writings and living a sacred life. Therefore, notice those who are unruly and are manifesting their own opinions and causing division. Stay away from them.

Listen, in this era it will look like those following the Scriptures are the ones causing the divisions and trouble, but anyone teaching and living the Scriptures will cause problems for those who are following their own opinions or the world's view. How do you know the difference? Study the word! How do you know whose interpretation is correct? Let Scripture interpret scripture. It is not that difficult if you are truly reading and studying the Word. Most of Scripture is very clear without any interpretation. Those who use the idea that there are many interpretations as an argument usually cannot support their opinion by the Scriptures. II Timothy 2:15 says, "to study to show yourself approved unto God. A worker not being ashamed but rightly teaching and living the Word." Further, you cannot follow Scripture and tradition. They will be in conflict at some point. Stay with Scripture. Be careful at following just one person. Even if that person is designated as the one overall

Philippians—The Path to Joy!

leader of religion. If his statements contradict Scripture, you must follow Scripture. What if this is the religion that your grandma, mom, and all of your family was and is in? If it contradicts scripture, you have to walk away from it. That is precisely what Paul did. Stand firm in the Word of God that is written in the book we call the Bible.

² Resolving differences has to do with thinking through the problems based upon the Lord, which means looking to the Scriptures to resolve problems and differences between each other. The Greek rendering in this verse actually says, "think the same thoughts." God's word should determine your thinking. If His Word determines your thinking, then, you will think the same way about issues. The problem is that people hold on to their opinions about issues. We live in the era that is called postmodernism. The postmodern thought is that everybody has their own truth and their own opinion. We are to accept everyone's opinion and truth, but the reality of such an idea is that it divides those who truly are following God's Word, because it is all about His truth and not our own opinions. Therefore, the believer in Christ is to follow God's Word and not his own opinion and not his own truth. God's truth prevails. Syntyche is a person in the church. Some translations translate this differently, but careful examination interprets this as a leader in the church.

³ The Christian life is to be filled with pristine clear crisp joy. This joy is to be of the purest and sincerest happiness found by mankind. It is a command and is to be of the act of the will. Rejoice in the Lord. The reason for this type of happiness is based on the grace of the Lord Jesus Christ. He has given freely the opportunity to have your sin debt paid for by Himself. He has freely offered all of the blessings in the Heavenly places and those who have responded to Christ are the recipients of such grace and blessings. Your sin debt is paid for and you have been granted the righteousness of Christ. There is much to rejoice about. The Lord is reason for a happy

Philippians—The Path to Joy!

heart. The heart is to be in a state of rejoicing no matter the circumstances of life.

[4] The Greek word used for yieldingness is *epieikēs*. It is a difficult word to translate into English. Many different words have been used to convey the meaning, such as sweet reasonableness, generosity, goodwill, friendliness, charity toward the faults of others, mercy toward the failures of others, indulgence of the failures of others, leniency, moderation, forbearance, gentleness, and yieldingness. Many prefer sweet reasonableness. Others prefer using graciousness. In the JEN translation, yieldingness is used because the root word of *epieikēs means to yield*. The word is a powerful word and if you applied it to your life, it would remedy many problems. The two top characteristics of a Christian should be humility and yielding up your rights. If you put those two together, you have a man or woman who is humbly walking with God and not demanding rights but yielding to others. Why would you do this? Because that is what humility does. The proudful are demanding. The proudful are the angry ones. The proudful will get what they want one way or another, but this is not godliness. Pride does not lead to Christ likeness. God is most glorified in you when Christ is most exemplified through you. Humility causes God to respond to the believer by providing extra grace (James 4:6). Therefore, as you humble yourself to God and yield your rights to others, God provides you with more grace to go through your immediate problems. The Lord is near, Paul writes. God is in your presence working on your behalf. He is working in you to give you inner strength. His grace will power you through your problems. His grace gives you emotional and spiritual stability. Focusing on yourself, demanding your rights, and consumed with self-love and self-esteem produces emotional instability and anxieties. The root of anxieties is fear. The antidote to fear is love. Grow in love displaying the qualities of love, and you will be on your way toward emotionally stability. (See I John 4:18).

Philippians—The Path to Joy!

[5] The Greek grammar for anxious is in the present imperative. It is a command to stop being anxious. Right now, in real time, if you are anxious, God says to stop. It is a command. This verse is one of the verses that enabled me to understand that anxiety is a choice. God would never have commanded you to stop being anxious if it was a medical condition. Anxiety is a temptation, and you have the ability to say no to it. Anxiety is based upon perception that produces a chemical imbalance. Thus, the medical condition is produced because of faulty thinking. If you change the way you think and base your thinking on facts and truth, you will reverse, eventually, the chemical imbalances in your brain. This will enable you to manage your anxieties. What about those who say that anxiety is not a sin? Well, they could be meaning that anxiety is a temptation, and you can't stop from the trigger introducing anxiety. If that is what they mean, they are correct. All temptation is triggered in the thoughts and then it is what you do with it that becomes sin or not. God never says be anxious, and do not sin. He says do not be anxious.

What is the antidote for anxiousness? God says in verse six to firstly, to stop being anxious. Secondly, He says to pray. The word pray is a general word meaning to worship God. It means to pray, praise, exult, exalt, and such. Thirdly, God says to supplicate. Supplication generally is used in the Scriptures to pray for others and to have others pray for you. Paul is calling on the body of Christ to support each other when faced with anxieties. Here it is most likely used with similar meanings. When you are anxious, pray for others. Ask others to pray for you. Intensify your prayers. It is always good to intensify what we know are the solutions when we are challenged with difficult situations. Fourthly, Paul says to give thanks in everything. When you are anxious, thank God that He is in control. Thank Him that He has the solutions. Thank Him for the trial and the situation. Thank Him for the experience you are going through. Thank Him for the lessons you are learning. Thank Him

Philippians—The Path to Joy!

that this life is not the end, but the next life is what you are being prepared for through this experience. Lastly, Paul says let your request be known to God. Pray exactly what you need God to do for you. At this point, be precise. Write out this prayer request in your prayer journal.

⁶ The source of your peace is God. His peace is greater than your mind. God is pointing out even though the battle is in the mind, His peace excels your mind. You must use your mind to conquer anxiety, but God's peace is superior to your mind. The true source of finding freedom from all anxieties is God giving you peace. Are unbelievers able to find freedom from anxieties? Absolutely. "Change your thinking, change your life." However, the peace that a believer in Christ Jesus the Lord can experience far exceeds anything that a non-Christian will ever experience. God's peace surpasses the ability of man's capability of gaining this sweet peace. God's peace is a guardian of the heart and perceptions. The word perception is used based on the Greek word used in the text. The Greek word for thoughts or perceptions is νόημα. It is derived from the root word νοέω, which means perception. Anxieties are based upon fear. Fear is the root of anxieties. Anxieties are produced when the brain is triggered to think about "what if" type questions. The brain is triggered by perceptions rather than reality. Because it is not a fight or flight mode, the fear chemicals stay activated in the brain and produce a continuous flow of anxieties. The solution is to guard your thought process from perceptions and make yourself look at the facts and respond to the facts according to Scripture. This is one reason it is so important to be studying the Bible on a daily basis so that you are able to look for the proper Scriptures that correspond with your present problem and respond biblically. This honors God. It brings a peace of mind to you.

⁷ Paul is giving his last few thoughts as he begins to conclude his letter. He commands them to take an inventory or to calculate what is excellent and worthy of praise. Your thoughts are to be

Philippians—The Path to Joy!

obsessed with the good. The whole list that Paul writes in verse eight is about thinking intensely of wholesome thoughts. Read the list. Concentrate on these types of things in your thinking. Your brain will naturally gravitate to the bad. You must use your mind inside you to train your brain to think on what is good. You will never get to the place where you can coast along in the Christian life. You have to work at thinking about good things. You have to reject the bad thoughts. You will be introduced to bad thinking so reject those thoughts. Redirect your brain to the good. Be prepared with information or Bible verses that you can quickly redirect your brain. The battle is in your thoughts. Bring every thought captive to Christ.

[8] The Christian life is a life of discipline. Godly thinking and godly behavior go together. Therefore, Paul in verse eight encourages them to think in a godly manner. Now in verse nine, he encourages them to live in a godly manner. Emotional and spiritual stability is derived from a well-disciplined life of obedience to God's Word. You must learn the Word, receive it into your heart, and practice it as a normal routine. Paul stated to the church at Philippi that they learned and received the way to live, and they heard about it from others and saw it in Paul's life. He modeled it for them. Now he exhorts them to make what they heard, received, and saw a part of their daily living. What will be the results? Not only peace, but God will be with them. You will have both His presence and His peace if you live the Scriptures. What happens if you don't live the Scriptures? You will not have peace. You will have confusion. You will have stress and worry. Discipline your life so that you live as the Latin term *Coram Deo* expresses. It means to live in the presence of God, under His authority, and for His glory. Further, the result will be as Isaiah 32:17 says, "the result of living right will be peace, and the effort of living right leads to rest and stability forever" (JEN).

Philippians—The Path to Joy!

[9] Contentment is the great character trait of a Christian. The contentment rests in Christ. You are to be content with Christ and what He has provided for you. You are to be content with your purpose and place in life. Your priority is to glorify God. Therefore, you must work at that responsibility and leave the results to God. Paul says he learned contentment. You, too, have to learn how to be content. You rely on the Holy Spirit to enable you to discover this great character trait. Trust that God is Jehovah Jireh. He is the God who provides. Trust Jesus to provide for your every need. Tell Him what you need. Thank Him for His past provisions. Thank Him for His past grace. Know that He will provide future grace as well. Many people feel as through God has let them down. Maybe you are one of them. What do you do with that thought? You realize that all of us have felt and thought that same thing. You begin to change your thinking about that by looking at what the Bible says. God is to be trusted even when it seems like He does not care at all. I Peter 5:7 says to cast all of your problems on God because He cares for you. You will never feel like God cares until you truly give Him your problems and leave them with Him. Trust him to work out the problems His way and in His time. Life is not about you. It is about God and His glory, as hard as that is to hear and grasp. Life is not about being happy. It is about being obedient to the true and living God.

[10] The Greek word for initiated is μυέω which is translated in some versions of the Bible as learn or secret. It does mean to initiate and is in the perfect passive, which means it is something initiated by someone else and has begun with continuous results. God has initiated this learning process with Paul to teach him how to be content and satisfied in all circumstances that he might find himself in because of serving Jesus. This is an important notation that God will initiate the work in your life. As with Paul, likewise, it will be with you, at times, painful. At times life will be good. At times life will be extremely difficult. God desires for you to learn how to be

Philippians—The Path to Joy!

content and happy in Christ, not in circumstances. If you focus on your pain, you will find it difficult to trust Him. You will find it difficult to be a godly man or woman. You have to keep your eyes on the Author and Finisher of your faith—Jesus. If you are a believer in Christ, you are an ambassador of Christ. You represent another kingdom. You are to represent His policies and regulations found in the Scriptures. That is all you are authorized to live by and to hold out to others. In verse 13 of this chapter, God gives insight doe how you are able to be content in all circumstances.

[11] This is a classic verse that is quoted quite a lot in Christianity. You can do all things through Christ. But to clarify what God is saying. Firstly, you can do all things through Christ means that whatever God is permitting to happen in your life, He will sustain you in it. Doing all things does not mean whatever you want or desire. It means primarily whatever state you find yourself in for the service of Christ, you can do it through Jesus. Secondly, the Greek word "en" is translated "by" Christ, or "in" Christ, or through Christ. At times, it is instrumental, but in this verse, it is to be used as a state or a position. In other words, Christ is empowering the believer because of the connection the believer has with Christ. He is in the believer through the Person of the Holy Spirit. That connection empowers the believer to go through the period of hardship. He pours His grace in the believer in a super abundant manner giving the believer the ability to keep on going. Therefore, look to Jesus for strength. Ask Him for grace. Humble yourself under His authority and let Him empower you. You may not feel power. you don't feel grace. You just feel the pressures of the difficulty, but you trust that the Lord Jesus is empowering you through this difficulty.

[12] We need each other. Partner up with other believers to help you through the Christian life. Find safe Christians who truly believe in Jesus and His Word. Share together. Pray together. Pray for one

Philippians—The Path to Joy!

another. Confess your sins to one another and pray for each other. Be what a church is to be.

[13] Paul is just continuing his thought about how this church supplied his needs. He is not putting down the other churches who did not supply. He is simply thanking them for their giving. Just be thankful for what people do for you. Be content in all situations. Don't expect anything. When it happens, be thankful for what they did, no matter how large or small.

[14] Paul is being clear that he was not after the gift. He wanted them to multiply in the results of their giving. This means that there are rewards on earth and Heaven for being obedient to the Scriptures. Jesus taught in Matthew 6 to lay up treasures in Heaven by your giving to the needs of others here on earth. Be conscious of the needs of others and give to others. You might think that you don't have enough money to give to others, but think twice. It is better to give than to receive. We all have something that we can give. Give to God what is His. Give to the needs of others. If you do, you will be bearing fruit both here and later. Giving helps you to get your eyes of off yourself and onto the Lord Jesus and others. Giving is gaining rewards in Heaven. Many people say they don't want to serve for the purpose of rewards, but this is incorrect thinking. The Bible has much to say about working for rewards. Further, the more rewards you have, the more glory the Lord Jesus receives from your labors here on earth.

[15] As in verse 13, this is not instrumental but because of the union with Christ, the believer is in a state, position, or connection with Christ that Jesus is providing the grace to meet whatever the need is in the present moment. This verse is not speaking of someday in Heaven, but rather in the future, here on earth as a believer has needs Jesus will provide. He is Jehovah Jireh—God my provider. This is all based upon the covenant relationship the believer has with God through Jesus Christ the Lord.

Philippians—The Path to Joy!

[16] Life is all about Jesus Christ and His glory. Life is not centered around people. The sooner you understand that and align your life to that goal, the happier you will be in life. Your happiness and fulfillment is in direct proportion to you centering your life around the Lord Jesus Christ. It is a paradox. The more you give your life to Him, the more you gain.

[17] God never refers to a believer in Christ as a sinner. He calls His people saints. It is from the Greek word ἅγιος, which means to be set apart or to be sacred. Believers in Christ are consecrated to God. They are separated from the world to God. The significance is that as Christian, you are not viewed by God as a sinner. You still will sin while on this earth, but you are viewed as one who has been redeemed, cleansed, purified, and have a holy position before God. If you are able to grasp Paul's argument about sin in Romans 7, you will understand that when a Christian does sin, it is not his true new nature that sins. "But now I am no longer the one sinning, but the indwelling sin in me" (Romans 7:17 JEN). Your new nature can't sin, but the indwelling sin still can and does.

[18] Paul's benediction consists of blessing them with God's Grace through Jesus Christ the Lord. Everyone needs to be covered by the grace of the Lord Jesus. It is His favor, strength, blessings, provision, and approval, which is unearned. Grace is simply freely given by God to His people. How do you get more grace? 1. Prayer (Hebrews 4:16), 2. Word of God (Acts 20:32), 3. Humility (James 4:6-10). Peter says to grow in the grace and knowledge of the Lord Jesus (II Peter 3:18). You need the cover of grace over your life. His grace will strengthen you and empower you through difficult times. His grace will keep you sweet. His grace will protect you from bitterness.

Made in the USA
Monee, IL
27 January 2020